100+ Free & Cheap Things to do in Atlanta with Kids

Copyright 2011
Sue Rodman

# Introduction

*Field Trips with Sue* is a regional travel blog about things to do with kids in Atlanta and the Southeast. It covers outings, day trips, weekend getaways and vacations to destinations of interest for families from the Atlanta area.

I have three boys, ages 13, 11 and 7. This book is a compilation of activities and fun we've discovered throughout the years. I've fact checked all of these entries, but it's still a good idea to contact the facility beforehand to ensure the deal is still available and confirm the details. I've given you websites and/or contact information so it should be easy to check before you go.

Some of the places profiled we've experienced as a family, and some are still on our list. If we've gone, you'll see more information and insight. If we haven't participated, you'll see what the website or promotional materials advertise.

For updates:

**Visit:** www.fieldtripswithsue.com

**Subscribe:** to *Field Trips with Sue* via email from www.fieldtripswithsue.com (click the upper right hand corner to subscribe and follow the directions, you must verify the subscription)

**Like:** *Field Trips with Sue* on Facebook: www.facebook.com/fieldtripswithsue

**Follow:** *Field Trips with Sue* on Twitter: @suerodman

**Subscribe:** to *Field Trips with Sue*'s Youtube Channel: www.youtube.com/suerodman

I hope this book helps create lasting memories for you and your family. Let me know if you have suggestions, ideas or comments.

Sincerely,

Sue Rodman

This book is dedicated to my faithful field trip companions:

Paul, Nicholas, Sam and Jake

# Contents

# ~ Events at Retail Locations ~

There are several retail establishments in the Atlanta area that entice customers by offering free workshops or programs for children. Events are held in the store on a certain day and/or timeframe. There is no purchase required to participate in these programs, but chances are, you'll leave with something! It's always a good idea to visit the store's website or contact the location closest to you to make sure the events are happening.

## Summer Reading Programs

Each summer several organizations offer incentives to get children to read. We've been introduced to several different book series through these programs that have become family favorites including: *Magic Tree House, Percy Jackson* and *39 Clues*. If you have a local book store nearby, ask if they offer a summer reading program for kids. Chances are, they do!

## Check it Out Reading

This program is done through the Atlanta Spirit, the parent company of the Atlanta Hawks and Atlanta Thrashers. Kids grades K-12 read five books and receive a bookmark and youth ticket to an Atlanta Hawks and Atlanta Thrashers game. The program is available June 1 at local libraries and runs into August.

## Barnes and Noble Summer Reading Program

**Web:**  http://www.barnesandnoble.com/summerreading/index.asp

Students in grades 1-6 read eight books and receive a FREE book from a pre-determined list.

# Borders Summer Reading Program

**Web:**  http://www.borders.com/

In the past, Borders has done a summer reading program as well. At press time, the stores I called could not guarantee the program would be in place, but assumed it would happen. Contact the Borders or Waldenbooks near you to see if they are hosting a summer reading program.

# Wren's Nest Critter t-shirts

**Web:**  http://bit.ly/le7pNx

Read five Brer Rabbit stories, fill out a form available online and receive a Brer Fox, Brer Rabbit, Brer Terrapin or Brer Lion t-shirt. Read five more stories and earn another tee. Read twenty stories total to collect all four! If you don't have any Brer Rabbit stories, you can purchase them at the Wren's Nest gift shop or online at http://wrensnest.bigcartel.com/.

# Little Shop of Stories Summer Reading Program

**Web:**  http://littleshopofstories.com/events.php

This is an independent children's bookstore in Decatur that offers a summer reading challenge to read 40 hours over the summer. Children receive prizes for each 10 hours they read. At the end of the summer, there is a celebratory pizza party for those that reach the 40 hour goal.

# Your local library

**Web:**  http://www.georgialibraries.org/public/summerreading.php

Most local libraries offer a summer reading program with prizes for reaching different goals. Our local library has offered books, milkshakes and even kid's meals at the local Chick-fil-A.

# Bass Pro Shops Camps

**What:** Family Summer Camp and holiday camps

**Where:** Bass Pro Shops, 5900 Sugarloaf Pkwy
Lawrenceville (678-847-5500)

**When:** Contact the store for details or watch the
advertising circulars and website

**Web:** http://www.basspro.com

Bass Pro Shops offer family camp several times a year that includes lots of fun activities for kids. In the past their big camps have been over the summer and their Holiday Winter Wonderland in November and December. Each camp has something a little unique (like Santa at Christmas or the Easter Bunny in the spring) all include games, crafts, workshops and prizes geared toward children. We went to the summer camp last year and it was even more fun than I anticipated. The boys shot arrows, cast fishing line trying to hit the big mouth bass buckets and enjoyed the shooting arcade.

# Lego Mini-Build

**Where:** LEGO Store Discover Mills Mall
5900 Sugarloaf Pkwy
Lawrenceville (678-847-6078)

**When:** First Tuesday of the Month
beginning at 5 pm

**Web:** http://bit.ly/iZVoBY

The LEGO Store at Discover Mills Mall in Lawrenceville hosts a monthly LEGO mini-build where children can build a mini-LEGO project that corresponds with the month – a flower for spring, a shamrock for St. Patrick's Day, a groundhog in February. This is a popular event, so expect to wait in line for your turn. When we went, it was about an hour wait, regardless of arrival time. Enterprising parents brought homework with them for kids to complete while they waited.

The store itself is pretty amazing!. There is a screen that scans a

LEGO set box and it virtually builds on the screen. As you move the box, the virtually built set moves. It was WAAYYY cool.

Take a look at this LEGO Mini-Build video (http://bit.ly/kBkH0z) to see if this is an activity for you. The only downside in my mind was the long wait, but if you aren't strapped for time, go for it and just come prepared.

## Lowe's Build and Grow Workshop

**Where:**     Any Lowe's Store

**When:**     Second and Fourth Saturday of Each Month at 10 am

**Web:**     https://www.lowesbuildandgrow.com/

Lowe's offers free kids workshops on the second and fourth Saturdays of the month. There is a three-step online registration process and as you go through the process, they'll tell you the Lowe's stores near you that offer the workshop. Pictures of the crafts are on the website, too. Lowe's provides all the materials and tools and gives each child a kid-sized apron.

## Home Depot Workshop

**Where:** Any Home Depot Store

**When:** First Saturday of Every Month, 9 – 12 pm

**Web:**    http://bit.ly/lxO8JR

The first Saturday of every month, Home Depot sets aside a corner of the store for kids to hammer and glue a wooden craft. We've made treasure boxes, flower pots, fire engines, and airplanes, to name a few. My kids have always loved coming home and painting their projects. Children receive a kid's size Home Depot apron, a craft kit to build on site, certificate, and pin.

# Michael's Craft Programs

**Where:**        Michael's Craft Stores

**When:**         Search the store closest to you and click on "events"

**Web:**          http://bit.ly/j6B9rG

Michael's Craft Stores offer free Make it and Take it Crafts in stores across the country. Generally the program is on Saturday but the dates and times change, so check the website. In order to find out what is happening near you, visit the Michael's website and search by zip code. Then, click events. Some of the events are free, others may require a purchase but the crafting supplies are provided.

# Lakeshore Learning Crafts

**Where:**        Lakeshore Learning

**When:**         Saturdays from 11 am – 3 pm

**Web:**          http://bit.ly/jMaPcW

Lakeshore Learning has a wonderful craft program that is designed for children 3 and up. I took my boys when they were preschoolers and they loved it. It doesn't take long and it's just a reason to get out of the house and get moving – especially if it's a rainy day. On some Saturdays we'd do this and then head to Home Depot for their workshop, too.

# The American Girl Store

**Where:** American Girl Stores at Northpoint Mall
1202 North Point Circle
Alpharetta (877-247-5223)

**When:** Various dates and times
See site for details

**Web:**    http://bit.ly/lGTC5w

The American Girl Store at Northpoint Mall hosts several events in-store, including some free ones. The events are based on various dolls, including the Bitty Baby series for younger girls, and generally involve a craft. Note that not all of the events listed are free, but the free ones will say so in the description. Call the store for exact times.

## Pottery Barn Kids Book Club

**Where:**    Pottery Barn Kids Stores

**When:**    Every Tuesday 11 – 11:30 am

**Web:**    http://bit.ly/kqQ4yr

Kids of all ages are invited to any Pottery Barn Kids store for story time every Tuesday. Members receive an official book club passport at their first story time and a special gift after attending five story times. There are special book club themes and occasional character appearances.

## Simon Mall Kidgits Club

**Where:**    Simon Malls including: Town Center at Cobb, Gwinnett Place, Discover Mills and Mall of Georgia

**When:**    Various events throughout the year

**Web:**    http://www.simon.com/kidgits/

**Cost:**    Some Simon Kidgit Club events are free for everyone, others are free for members. Membership is $5 annually per child.

Simon Malls Kidgits Club has lots of fun activities for toddlers, pre-schoolers and young elementary students. Events and activities vary by season and could include parties with safe summer or back to school theme. Seasonal events like the Boo Bash or the visit with Santa are also popular. Some events feature favorite characters like Handy Manny or Minnie Mouse. Visit the Simon Malls Kidgits Club website for the mall near you and a list of upcoming events. Join online or at your first event.

# REI's Family Adventure Program

**Where:**      Download a guide online

**When:**       Anytime

**Web:**        http://www.rei.com/family-adventure

REI has a good summer adventure guide to help your children (and you) get outside and really take in the world around you. When kids complete the adventure, they receive a certificate for their efforts. Not sure where to go on your adventure? REI has a list of family friendly hiking and biking spots on the site, as well.

# Useful Links:

**American Girl Store Video:** http://bit.ly/lf9XMs

# ~ Museums & Attractions ~

Atlanta has many fantastic museums geared toward children. Some of the museums offer free admission, while others have specific days, times, or promotions for free entry. For museums with free days, some restrictions apply and can change without notice, so call before you go. Remember, those free days can be more crowded than other days, so factor that in to your schedule!

## The Georgia Aquarium

**Where:** 225 Baker St. NW, Atlanta (404-581-4000)

**When:** Your Birthday!

**Web:** http://www.georgiaaquarium.org/happy-birthday.aspx

The Georgia Aquarium is one of the most loved of Atlanta's attractions. To visit for free, take advantage of the free Birthday Visit at the Georgia Aquarium. Just show a picture ID with your birthday on it and Georgia residents are admitted for free on their special day. The Aquarium also has kids' free days throughout the year in conjunction with fun holidays and promotions. These dates were not set at press time, but watch Aquarium social media channels for details. In 2010 they offered promotions such as free admission for children dressed like a pirate or princess.

Note the free admission is only for a general admission ticket. This ticket allows admission into the five main galleries: Cold Water Quest, Georgia Explorer, Ocean Voyager, Tropical Diver and River Scout. My favorite animals are the otters, the seaweed looking fish and those HUGE crabs that look like something from a sci-fi movie.

There is an additional ticket for the Deepo 4-D theatre and the new AT&T Dolphin Tales show. These tickets are not free on your birthday. Know the children you are going with before purchasing additional tickets for the 4-D movie. Keeping the 3-D glasses on my preschooler was hard enough, but when the rain came down and the chair jumped under him, it was a bit much. That said, the older kids loved it.

## Zoo Atlanta

**What:** Family Pass to Zoo Atlanta

**Where:** 800 Cherokee Ave., SE, Atlanta
(404-624-9453)
You must check out the Zoo Atlanta pass at your local library prior to going to the Zoo

**When:** Whenever the pass isn't already checked out

**Web:** http://bit.ly/mEhft9

If you have a library card in Georgia, you can check out a free family pass to Zoo Atlanta! There are limitations. The pass can only be checked out for seven days, once a year per family. It cannot be renewed and you cannot put a hold on it. Patrons need to bring the pass and their library receipt to the window at the Zoo Atlanta for admission for up to four people.

My local library recommends calling first to see if the pass is available for checkout. As you might expect, it's a popular item, especially in the summer, so if you have trouble securing the pass, try again in the winter or off times of the year such as September.

# Imagine It! The Children's Museum of Atlanta

**What:** Target Free Day

**Where:** The Children's Museum of Atlanta
275 Centennial Olympic Park Dr. NW
Atlanta (404-659-5437)

**When:** Second Tuesday of Every Month
from 1pm – 7 pm.

**Web:** http://bit.ly/kYBkbn

The second Tuesday of the month, Target Stores sponsors a free day at Imagine It! The Children's Museum of Atlanta. Free days for 2011 are: June 14, July 12, Aug. 9, Sept. 13, Oct. 11, Nov. 8 and Dec. 13.

While you are at Imagine It, be sure to pick up a When I am... card that corresponds to your child's age. The When I am cards offer suggestions on how to help your child get the most out of the museum. We all know children learn through play, but these cards help you understand what they are learning. It also gives you specific information on what you can expect from a child at that age and additional resources to learn more.

# Woodruff Arts Center

**What:** Target Family Thursdays

**Where:** Woodruff Arts Center
1280 Peachtree St. NE
Atlanta (404)733-4200)

**When:** First four Thursdays in September
(Sept. 1, 8, 15 and 22, 2011)

**Web:** http://bit.ly/iLf6ZQ

The Woodruff Arts Center encompasses the High Museum of Art, Atlanta Symphony Orchestra, Alliance Theatre and Young Audiences, a consortium of arts available for school programs, festivals and other educational events. The Woodruff Arts Center is partnering with Target Corporation to host Target Family Thursdays in September. Details were not complete at press time, but there will be a variety of activities that are either free or for a reduced price. Events will be all day and into the evening. Contact the Woodruff Arts Center for the latest information.

## High Museum of Art: Fulton Free Days

**Where:** High Museum of Art, 1280 Peachtree St. NE, Atlanta (404-733-4444)

**When:** First Saturday of the Month

**Web:** http://bit.ly/ivR94y

On the first Saturday of every month, the High Museum of Art welcomes Fulton County residents to the Museum for free. You must show proof of residency. Students attending college or university in Fulton County are also eligible with their valid college ID. The tickets allow entrance to see the current exhibits, as well as the permanent collections.

There are several reasons to take children to the High and the Greene Family Gallery is a big one. The gallery is a great place for smaller children to get out of the stroller and play. They can draw; create a sculpture from trash as Howard Finster did; build a museum of their own like High architect Richard Meir; create a puppet show; dress up using scarves; or play in the life-sized block mats.

## High Museum of Art: Discovery Backpacks

**What:** Discovery Backpacks

**Where:** High Museum of Art
1280 Peachtree St. NE
Atlanta (404-733-4444)

**When:** Free with Admission

**Web:** http://bit.ly/mJVvuy

Parents won't want to miss checking out Discovery Backpacks (free with museum admission). This is a memorable and fun way to introduce your children (and yourself) to some of the classic pieces in the High's permanent collection.

There are two versions of the backpacks, each with four lucite cards depicting a piece in the museum along with questions to ask and accompanying objects that make it hands-on. For example, one card features a marble statue of a girl. You go to that floor, open your backpack and pull out the book "Escape from Pompeii." Read the book in front of the statue, then, answer the questions on the card. Questions like, "What do you think the weather is like?" Answer: "Windy, her dress is billowing." Then you pull out the blocks of stone, wood, and marble and choose the material used to make this statue. My then 4-year-old enjoyed this and I was surprised at how accurate his answers were. Another card asks kids to interpret a painting of two circles and a swish underneath. I saw suns, not very creative. My oldest saw two people hugging each other. I love that painting now and whenever I see it, I think of him and smile.

The Discovery Backpacks make the art more accessible and the museum less overwhelming, while adding that hands-on element that kids (and adults) crave.

## Center for Puppetry Arts Museum

**Where:** 1404 Spring St. NW, Atlanta
(404-873-3089)

**When:** Thursdays from 1 – 3 pm and first
Sat. of every month
for Fulton Co. Residents

**Web:** http://bit.ly/lV9KJ6

The Center for Puppetry Arts is a gem in Atlanta. If you haven't been, it needs to be on your list. Visit the Center for Puppetry Arts Museum for free on Thursdays from 1-3 pm. A life-sized Big Bird greets you as you enter the Henson Gallery. Videos show how Jim Henson changes the emotion of a puppet and even how puppets are used to create the TV show "Sid the Science Kid". My son loves creating his own puppet faces using the features and heads at an interactive station.

In addition to Jim Henson puppets, the Center has a unique gallery showcasing different types of puppets. In certain areas, kids can work the puppets themselves. Warning: even though kids love this area once they get used to it, they can be a little scared walking in.

Residents of Fulton County, Ga. enjoy Free Museum Saturdays, the first Saturday of every month. Fulton County residents, students attending a school in Fulton County, and Fulton County government employees with proper I.D. receive free admission to the museum exhibitions. Admission does not include performances or workshops. Eligible participants may purchase tickets for performances and workshops on Free Museum Saturdays at a 25% discount, subject to availability.

# Fernbank Science Center

**What:** Fernbank Science Center
(NOT Fernbank Museum
of Natural History)

**Where:** Fernbank Science Center
156 Heaton Park Dr., NE, Atlanta
(678-874-7102)

**When:** Hours vary, check the website

**Web:** http://fsc.fernbank.edu/

**Cost:** Admission is Free, Planetarium Shows
are $4 Adults, $3 Students and Seniors

The Fernbank Science Center, not the Fernbank Museum of Natural History, offers exhibit halls, the Fernbank Forest, as well as a planetarium.

Among the permanent exhibits in the exhibit hall are portrayals of the natural environment and vanishing habitats of Georgia, featuring mounted taxidermy specimens. Astronomy displays include Fernbank's meteorite collection and an authentic Apollo spacecraft.

Outside guests can walk through the Fernbank Forest, a 65-acre old-growth forest representing one of the last remaining enclaves of the original Piedmont forest in the southeast. The protected forest is home to many animal and plant species native to the area.

In addition, there is a rose garden, a home composting demonstration site, rock and mineral walk and live chickens. The planetarium shows vary with the seasons.

This attraction definitely isn't as flashy as the better known Fernbank Museum of Natural History, but there's a lot to learn, the price is right, parking is free and it's a relaxing afternoon adventure away from the crowds.

# American Museum of Papermaking

**Where:** 500 10th St. NW
Atlanta, GA 30332 (404-894-6663)

**When:** Monday – Friday 9 – 5 pm

**Web:** http://ipst.gatech.edu/amp/

This museum in Midtown Atlanta traces the history of paper from 4000 B.C. to today's contemporary paper artists. It is associated with the Georgia Institute of Technology and includes workshops as well as exhibits.

# CDC Global Health Odyssey Museum

**Where:** 1600 Clifton Road, NE, Atlanta (800-232-4636)

**When:** Monday – Friday 9 – 5 pm w/extended hours on Thursday until 7 pm

**Web:** http://www.cdc.gov/museum/

The CDC museum is affiliated with the Smithsonian Institution and serves to educate visitors about the CDC, public health and the benefits of prevention. In addition to permanent exhibits, the museum hosts traveling exhibits and a cool camp called Disease Detective Camp. The camp is designed for juniors and seniors in high school to explore careers in public health. If you are interested in the Disease Detective Camp, check the website for dates, times and pricing.

## Carter Center Library and Museum

**Where:** 441 Freedom Parkway, Atlanta (404-865-7100)

**When:** Mon. – Sat. 9 – 4:45 pm, Sun. 12 – 4:45 pm

**Web:** http://www.jimmycarterlibrary.gov/museum/

**Cost:** Children 16 and under are free, Adults $8

The Museum of the Jimmy Carter Library includes photographs and historical memorabilia from the Carter presidency (1976-1981). An exact replica of the Oval Office and gifts received by the Carters are also featured. A permanent exhibit of significant events occurring during Jimmy Carter's life and political career includes photographs and artwork.

When you go, make sure to venture outside to the gardens and ponds. You can bring a fishing pole and fish in the stocked pond! You don't have to visit the museum to fish, just walk through the entry or around the Museum.

## State Capitol Tour and Museum

**What:** Tours of the Georgia State Capitol

**Where:** 214 State Capitol, Atlanta (404-463-4536

**When:** Varies by the time of year

**Web:** http://www.sos.ga.gov/archives/tours/about.html

The Georgia State Capitol is the center of government for the state, but it's also a historic building and is listed on the National Park Service's National Register of Historic Places. The stunning dome (the landmark that every kid notices from the highway) is made of real gold mined in Dahlonega, Ga. The Secretary of State's office hosts 20 minute orientation presentations, or if you plan ahead, you can request a 30 minute guided tour. Following the presentations, guests are welcome to visit the House and Senate and the Capitol Museum which are located on the 4th floor of the building. The tour and presentation begins on the second floor in the Capitol Rotunda where a guide provides an overview of the building and its history. Throughout the Capitol, visitors see a portion of the state's $2 million art collection, and stroll through the Hall of Valor, which houses the state's historic flag collection.

# Federal Reserve Bank of Atlanta

**Where:** 1000 Peachtree St. NE
Atlanta (404-498-8764)

**When:** Mon. – Fri. 9:30 am, 11 am and 1 pm for group guided tours (must be prearranged)
Self-Guided Tours (for those with less than 10 people) are Mon.-Fri. 9 – 4 pm

**Web:** http://bit.ly/k8VySi

If your child is fascinated by money, here's a great museum and tour to show them the story of our monetary system (from barter to modern times) and teach them about the history of banking in America. They'll get to see examples of rare coins and currency and even go home with a bag of real shredded bills.

In addition to the tour, there are interactive and multimedia exhibits that provide an in-depth look at the role of the Federal Reserve including how they conduct monetary policy, and regulate and supervise banking. You can also get a look inside the cash-processing operations, where millions of dollars are counted, sorted, or shredded daily. The automated vault that uses robotics is fascinating to young and old.

Tours are free, but guided group tours of the museum (for groups of 10-30 people) must be prearranged and are by appointment only. Individuals and smaller groups can take a self-guided tour of the Visitors Center and Monetary Museum. Self-guided tours do not need to be scheduled.

## National Infantry Museum

**Where:** Fort Benning, 1775 Legacy Way
Columbus (706-685-5800)

**When:** Mon. – Sat. 9 – 5 pm, Sun. 11 – 5 pm

**Web:** http://www.nationalinfantrymuseum.com/

The National Infantry Museum tells the heroic story of everyday Infantrymen through a collection of more than 30,000 objects. It chronicles the journey from training through every conflict from before the Revolutionary War to action today in Iraq and Afghanistan. There is a special gallery recognizing Medal of Honor recipients and one that pays tribute to the family and loved ones the soldier leaves behind. Children will enjoy the play space and costumes available for role play in this gallery. The central exhibit, titled "The Last Hundred Yards" immerses the viewer in life-sized dioramas depicting the fight for the last hundred yards of some of the toughest battles throughout US history. Behind the museum is an authentically recreated World War II Company Street. Each of the seven buildings is furnished with period pieces and includes audio recordings of life on an Army post during the 1940s.

Although admission is free to the museum, there are extra experiences that charge a nominal fee. For $5, guests can fire weapons in a training simulator, just like the one used by the soldier's training at Fort Benning. There is also an IMAX Theatre where movies range from $6 – $8.

# Waffle House Museum

**Where:**        2719 East College Ave., Decatur (770.326.7086)

**When:**         Noon – 3 pm June 4 and July 9, 2011
                  (or call to make an appointment for another day)

**Web:**          http://bit.ly/l3qnai

Love Waffle House? Well, now you can visit the place where it all started. The Waffle House® Museum is the site of the very first Waffle House® restaurant. It opened back in 1955 after two neighbors, Joe Roger, Sr. and Tom Forkner, decided Avondale Estates needed a 24-hour restaurant. Today, the chain they started has 1600 restaurants in 25 states. The restaurant has been restored to feel as though you are stepping back into 1955. In addition to the restaurant, the museum features Waffle House memorabilia from the past 54 years.

Although I have not been to the museum, it looks like kids can play restaurant cooking with make believe steak and eggs and serve customers from behind the counter.

If you sign up on the web to be a "Regular", you'll receive information on when the museum will be open, as well as coupons.

# Margaret Mitchell Playhouse and Antique Funeral Museum

**Where:**        168 N. McDonough Street, Jonesboro (770-478-7211)

**When:**         Mon. – Sun. 9 – 5 pm

**Web:**          http://bit.ly/kMBMlv

Housed on the grounds of Pope Dickson & Son Funeral Home, the antique funeral museum displays a horse-drawn hearse, a pre-Civil War casket and antique Civil War embalming equipment. On the grounds is a playhouse where future author Margaret Mitchell played as a child.

# Marietta Fire Museum

**What:** A Fire Station in your community and/or Marietta Fire Museum

**Where:** 112 Haynes Street, Marietta (770-794-5491)

**When:** Mon. – Fri. 8 – 5 pm

**Web:** http://1.usa.gov/lO7WUt

Little boys (and girls) are fascinated by fireman and fire trucks. A great free activity in any community is a visit to the local fire station. The stations we've visited have let the boys climb on the trucks, wear the fire hats, and even try on the boots! It's always nice to bring some treats for the firemen as a thank you or make a donation to the station.

If you have a real fireman fan, visit the Marietta Fire Museum. The museum has fire equipment dating back to the 1800s including fire service clothing, equipment and antique apparatus and, of course, fire trucks!

# Roswell Fire and Rescue Museum

**Where:**        RFD Station 1, 1002 Alpharetta St., Roswell, Ga. (770-641-3730)

**When:**        Open 7 days in the day and early evening Except when crew is on a call

**Web:**        http://bit.ly/lLTm7m

Here's another fire and rescue museum, this time in Roswell. The main attraction for this museum is a 1947 Ford American LaFrance Pumper truck. This truck was the original fire truck used by the City of Roswell. This unique truck is often seen in parades around Atlanta. Bring your camera!

# Museum of Aviation

**Where:** GA Hwy 247 & Russell Pkwy
　　　　　Warner Robins (478-926-6870)

**When:** 9-5 pm Closed Easter, Thanksgiving,
　　　　　Christmas and New Year's Day

**Web:** http://www.museumofaviation.org/

This museum will thrill diehard aviation fans. They have more than 50 aircraft and exhibits that highlight World War II, The Korean War, Vietnam and the Ga. Aviation Hall of Fame.

# Phoenix Flies Celebration

**What:**　　　　　A Citywide Celebration of Living Landmarks

**Where:**　　　　Several locations around Atlanta

**When:**　　　　March 10-25, 2012

**Web:**　　　　　http://www.phoenixflies.org/index.php

The Atlanta Preservation Center sponsors this annual program that includes more than 150 events, from guided tours to lectures to open houses, at dozens of Atlanta's historic sites. Best of all, it's free!

Specific events change from year-to-year, so watch the website for a complete listing. In 2010, they had a fantastic line up for kids including guided tours and storytelling at the Wren's Nest, the home of Brer Rabbit author Joel Candler Harris; a tour of the Tullie Smith House and Farm at the Atlanta History Center; building a Box City; and a behind the scenes look at the Center for Puppetry Arts, where guests visited the Puppet Workshop where the puppets are designed and built and the Scene shop, where the scenery for the puppet shows is built.

For older kids and adults, there were several tours of Oakland Cemetery. Oakland is a fabulous place rich in local history. Several prominent Atlantan's are "residents" of Oakland including Margaret Mitchell, Bobby Jones, and Maynard Jackson. I've always wanted to take a tour of the architecturally stunning Fox Theatre, whose rescue in 1978 was the impetus for The Phoenix Flies celebration.

Some of the tours require reservations and many of the children's programs have limited availability, so check the Phoenix Flies website closer to the event for specific activities, dates and times, and whether or not you need reservations.

## Bank of America Museums on Us

**Where:**    150 Museums across the country

**When:**    First full weekend of the month

**Web:**    http://museums.bankofamerica.com/

If you're a Bank of America customer, your credit or debit card will get you in for free to more than 150 museums across the country including several in Georgia and Atlanta. At press time, Atlanta area museums participating in the program included The Atlanta History Center, High Museum of Art and the Jimmy Carter Presidential Library and Museum. Participating museums change, so check the Bank of America Museums on Us website before heading out – or call the museum's admissions desk and ask.

2011 Weekends include: June 4 & 5, July 2 & 3, August 6 & 7, September 3 & 4, October 1 & 2, November 5 & 6 and December 3 & 4.

## Smithsonian Museum Days

**Where:** Museums in Georgia and across the country

**When:** Saturday, Sept. 24, 2011

**Web:**    http://microsite.smithsonianmag.com/ museumday/

Smithsonian Magazine's annual Museum Day allows guests free admission to more than 1200 museums nationwide, including many in Georgia. An updated list comes out in June for the 2011 date, but Atlanta area museums that participated in 2010 include the High Museum of Art and Center for Puppetry Arts. To enter the museums for free, you must register and print out an admission card that becomes your ticket for the day.

Several of the museums offering free admission are in Cartersville, GA., which is about an hour north of Atlanta along I-75 toward Chattanooga, TN. These places are well worth the drive. Cartersville museums that participated in 2010 include: Tellus, the Northwest Georgia Science Museum, Booth Western Museum and Bartow History Museum . Cartersville is quite an unexpected cultural mecca. Our family has loved Tellus since it was the Weinman Mineral Museum. There are four galleries that cover dinosaur fossils, a mineral gallery (kids like interesting rocks!), Science in Motion and Collins Family Big Backyard (an interactive science play space), a planetarium, fossil dig, and gem panning. Download a Fossil Hunter license from the Tellus website and identify what you can find in the fossil dig area and a Treasure Map that helps identify the gemstones in the gem panning area. Both of these sheets are more for older kids that can read, but everyone will enjoy the activities.

# Blue Star Museums

| | |
|---|---|
| **Where:** | Across the US |
| **When:** | May 30, 2011 through Sept. 5, 2011 |
| **Web:** | http://www.bluestarfam.org/Programs/Blue_Star_Museums |

Blue Star Museums is a program that offers free admission to museums for all active duty, National Guard and Reserve military personnel and their families from Memorial Day through Labor Day. More than 1,100 museums have signed up for the 2011 Blue Star Museums program.

For a complete list of participating museums, see their website. Atlanta area museums include: The Breman Jewish Heritage and

Holocaust Museum, Michael C. Carlos Museum of Emory University, Marietta Museum of History, High Museum of Art, Heritage Sandy Springs Museum, Center for Puppetry Arts, CDC/Global Health Odyssey Museum.

# Helpful Links:

### Georgia Aquarium Free Birthday Program:
http://www.georgiaaquarium.org/happybirthday.aspx

### Imagine It! Children's Museum of Atlanta When I Am Cards:
http://www.childrensmuseumatlanta.org/parents/when

### Imagine It! Children's Museum of Atlanta
### Children learn through play:
http://www.childrensmuseumatlanta.org/parents/play

### The High Museum of Art's Greene Family Gallery:
http://bit.ly/ijqczD

### Fernbank Science Center Planetarium Shows:
http://fsc.fernbank.edu/planetarium.htm

### Tellus, Northwest Georgia Science Museum:
http://bit.ly/kcPxOP

### Booth Western Museum:
http://www.boothmuseum.org/

### Bartow History Museum:
http://www.bartowhistorymuseum.org/

# ~ Georgia Parks & Outdoors ~

On a bright and sunny Atlanta day, there is nothing better than enjoying a picnic lunch and a leisurely day at a playground or park. The following establishments offer something beyond just a playground and picnic table.

## Callaway Gardens

**Where:** 17800 Highway 27, Pine Mountain

**When:** January and February

**Web:** http://www.callawaygardens.com/

Callaway Gardens is about an hour and a half from downtown Atlanta and a great day trip, especially during January and February when admission is free! There are no coupons or special discounts to keep track of---Just show up!

Once you are there, enjoy the beautiful Cecil B. Day Butterfly Center and the Virginia Hand Callaway Discovery Center. The birds of prey show was on hiatus in 2011, but hopefully will be back in 2012. Bring bikes, or rent them on site and ride the Gardens' more than 10 miles of bike trails. We just enjoyed walking from the Discovery Center to the butterfly house. The boys played with turtles, rocks and sticks, watched fish in the creek and had a great time just running around.

# Piedmont Park

**Where:** Piedmont Park
1071 Piedmont Ave
Atlanta (404-876-4024)

**When:** Anytime

**Web:**   http://www.piedmontpark.org/

Atlanta is blessed with wonderful parks perfect for a free day of fun. In Midtown Atlanta, Piedmont Park offers many family friendly activities. In the summer, check out the Piedmont Park pool during free hours. Afterwards, meander through the park for more entertaining diversions.

Just outside the pool gates is a playground with soft cushioning underneath. Right next to the playground are level cement paths, perfect for bike riding, scooters or skates. If your child is just learning to ride a bike, this is a great place to practice.

On the way back to your car, walk across one of the bridges and stop to watch a mother duck and her ducklings dry themselves or a turtle sunning. The lake also offers good fishing. Across the bridge, is a large hill, perfect for rolling down. At the bottom, you may find dogs on their way to Piedmont Park's dedicated dog park. Outside the dog park is the Camp Market Garden. PPC Day Camp participants tend the garden and the produce is sold at the Saturday Green Market. The Green Market sometimes hosts children's activities for free or a nominal fee.

# Centennial Olympic Park

## Wednesday Wind Down

**Where:** Centennial Olympic Park Southern
Company Amphitheater
265 Park Ave. West NW
Atlanta (404-223-4499)

**When:** April – September 2011,
Wed. evenings 5:30 – 8 pm

**Web:**   http://bit.ly/lXg7bm

Centennial Olympic Park was built less than two decades ago for the 1996 Olympic Games. Not only is it our city's great legacy of a historical event but also a fantastic destination for families. April kicks off two free music programs, the Wednesday Wind Down and Music @ Noon. For a list of musicians, visit the website. On a warm spring or summer night, bring a picnic dinner and enjoy the music and other free attractions like the playgrounds or Fountain of Rings.

## Music @ Noon

**Where:** Centennial Olympic Park Southern
Company Amphitheater
265 Park Ave. West NW
Atlanta (404-223-4499)

**When:** April – September 2011
Tuesdays and Thursdays at Noon

**Web:**   http://www.centennialpark.com/events/man.html

In addition to the Wednesday Wind Down music series, Centennial Olympic Park offers the daytime Music @ Noon program. For a list of musicians, visit the website. Bring a picnic lunch and play on the two playgrounds at the other end of the park. When you get hot, cool off in the Fountain of Rings, or just watch the water show.

# Fourth Saturday Family Fun Days

**Where:**     Centennial Olympic Park, 265 Park Ave. West NW, Atlanta
               (404-223-4499)

**When:**      Fourth Saturday of each month
               May – September noon – 4 pm

**Web:**       http://www.centennialpark.com/events/fsffd.html

Enjoy an afternoon of free, themed events once a month from spring to fall at Centennial Olympic Park's Fourth Saturday Family Fun Day. The event is full of interactive, entertaining and educational activities for children and each Saturday features a different theme. The Park invites civic organizations, hobby enthusiasts, artisans, school groups and entertainers from around the Southeast to participate in the program. Fourth Saturday Family Fun Day is an award winning event, voted "Best Community Involvement" program in Georgia by the International Festivals and Events Association (IFEA).

Activities include educational programming, specialty workshops, touring shows, street performers, family-friendly performances, children's crafts, life-size chess games, appearances by on-air personalities, local sports mascots, contests, prizes, and more!

# See the Stars at Local Observatories

Who knew there were so many places to see the stars in Atlanta? Below is a round-up for amateur astronomers, or those of us who just like to look at the pretty night sky.

## Observatories: Georgia Tech Observatory

**Where:**     Georgia Tech Campus (404-385-8133)

**When:**      Contact Georgia. Tech for dates and times

**Web:**       http://www.astronomy.gatech.edu/

Georgia Tech has an observatory that is open to the public on certain nights, weather permitting. The Public Nights are contingent on clear weather, and it will be canceled if there are too many clouds, so check the website, www.astronomy.gatech.edu, before you go.

# Observatory: Fernbank Science Center

**Where:**        156 Heaton Park Dr., Atlanta (678-874-7102)

**When:**        Thursday and Friday evenings from 9 pm until 10:30 pm

**Web:**        http://fsc.fernbank.edu/observatory.htm

The Fernbank Observatory houses the largest telescope in the southeastern United States. Free public observations are offered every Thursday and Friday evening from 9 pm (or dark) until 10:30 pm (weather permitting). There is an astronomer available as well to position the telescope and answer questions.

# Observatory: Georgia Perimeter College Observatory

**What:**  Georgia Perimeter College, Dunwoody Campus

**Where:** 2101 Womack Rd., Atlanta (770-274-5000)

**When:** Second Saturday of the month

**Web:**    http://bit.ly/jpEWsR

Visitors can attend a monthly Open House at Georgia Perimeter College's Observatory. The Open House is the second Saturday of every month unless it rains. Visitors can also make an appointment for viewing anytime. Instructions are on the website. Note: This is a working scientific laboratory, so there is no heat, bathrooms, or refreshments.

# Observatories: Hard Labor Creek State Park

**Where:** 5 Hard Labor Creek Rd., Rutledge
(404-413-6024)

**When:** March – Oct. One Saturday a month

**Web:** http://www.chara.gsu.edu/HLCO/

Hard Labor Creek Observatory is open to the public one Saturday per month from March until October. In case of inclement weather, the facilities will still be open for a tour and a brief slideshow. Contact the GSU Department of Physics and Astronomy at least one week prior to the open house if you want to bring a large group. Public dates for 2011 are: June 11, July 9, August 6, September 17, and October 29. See the website for tour and observation times.

# Georgia State Parks

## Georgia State Parks: Library Pass

**Where:** All Over Georgia

**When:** Anytime with a Pass from the Library

**Web:** http://www.georgiastateparks.org/
www.georgialibraries.org

Planning a daytrip to the beach doesn't have to include an overnight stay at an oceanfront hotel; simply head to one of Georgia's State Parks free lakeside swimming beaches. A library card is all you need to check out a ParkPass or Historic Site Pass at Georgia's public libraries. The passes are good for free parking or admission at any of the 63 state parks and historic sites statewide.

With a diverse geographic topography, Georgia's state parks and historic sites offer adventures in northern mountains, midland swamplands, piedmont plains and along the beautiful Georgia coast. The State Parks are the best low-cost, high reward outing. In addition to self-discovery, there are planned programs that are either free or for a minimal cost. Check the Georgia State Park website for park activities near you.

## Georgia State Parks: Junior Ranger Program

**Where:** Georgia State Parks and Historic Sites

**When:** Anytime

**Web:** http://bit.ly/lWRDLe

The Georgia State Parks Junior Ranger program is a great way to engage with the outdoors, whether you're at a park or in the backyard. An activity book guides children (and parents) through a variety of activities that can be done at any of Georgia's State Parks and Historic Sites or even in their own backyard. As a parent, it helps me lend some structure to our outdoor adventures and gives us a place to start. Similar to scouting, Jr. Rangers receive badges based on the activities they complete.

Jr. Ranger activity books are available at any Georgia State Park. Activities in the book range from a water study to a historical timeline and are appropriate for any age. Children can do the activities by themselves or with an adult helper. Several State Parks offer ranger led programs around the various activities as well. To see the calendar of events for each park, visit the Georgia State Parks website. We've participated in activities such as tree climbing, fishing, historical demonstrations, and guided hikes.

# Georgia State Parks: Geo-Challenge

**Where:** Georgia State Parks

**Web:**   http://bit.ly/kQwF48

Geocaching is a high-tech treasure hunt that uses a GPS system to find a hidden box. To find the coordinates, register for free online at www.geocaching.com. When participants find the cache, they take a trinket from the box and leave one of their own. Some boxes contain stamps for participants to collect similar to a passport. There are geo-caches all around the world, and probably a few in your neighborhood.

In 2010, the Georgia State Parks created a geo-caching challenge in all 42 state parks where participants stamp a passport using stamps found in the caches. Passports can be obtained from any state park or downloaded from www.GeorgiaStatePark.org. The park service awards custom geo-coins for various levels of completion.

# Georgia State Parks: Free Entry Day

**Where:**          Georgia State Parks

**When:**           Sept. 25, 2011

**Web:**            http://www.georgiastateparks.org/FreeDay
(This is the same link they used in 2010. At press time it was not updated, so make sure it has the new information or go by the information below.)

On Sept. 25, Georgia State Parks are offering a free day as part of National Public Lands Day. We've covered several of Georgia's State Parks on *Field Trips with Sue* and have video of several park activities on our YouTube Channel. You can go to www.fieldtripswithsue.com and search Georgia State Parks or www.youtube.com/suerodman and search the park's name.

# National Parks Free Entrance Days

**Where:** All 392 National Parks

**When:** Fee free days in 2011 are: June 21, Sept. 24 and Nov. 11 – 13

**Web:** http://1.usa.gov/mhCDOj

Each year, the National Parks service hosts free entrance days, waving fees for all 392 National Parks across the country, including several in Georgia. I've visited the Augusta Canal National Heritage Area and loved it.

Make sure to check out the Junior Ranger Program at the National Parks, too. Kids can become Junior Rangers and earn patches by completing activities at selected parks. I didn't see any activities listed in Georgia, but there is also a web based Junior Ranger program (webrangers) where children play online games and earn virtual patches. I tested it with a program on the railroads and it was fun. Your child needs to be able to read in order to do most activities or have a parent's help. What a great way to prepare for a trip to a National Park!

# Silver Comet Trail

**What:** Riding Bikes, Walking, Rollerblading

**Where:** The Silver Comet Trail, 4342 Floyd Rd. Mableton (770-819-3279)
This is the address of the bike shop at the Floyd Rd. trail head

**Web:** http://www.silvercometga.com/

**Cost:** Free
(if you already have your bike or blades)

The Silver Comet Trail is located 13 miles northwest of Atlanta. It's free of charge, and travels west through Cobb, Paulding, and Polk counties. This quiet, non-motorized trail is for walkers, hikers, bicyclists, rollerbladers, dog walkers, and is wheelchair accessible.

The Trail is over 61 miles long, and starts near Mavell Road in Smyrna, Georgia. It ends at the Georgia/Alabama state line, near Cedartown and Esom.

At the Georgia/Alabama state line, the Silver Comet connects to the 33-mile long Chief Ladiga Trail. Both the Silver Comet Trail and Chief Ladiga are fully paved rail-trails built on abandoned railroad lines. The combined Silver Comet and Chief Ladiga trail length is estimated to be over 100 paved miles from Smyrna, Georgia to Anniston, Alabama.

We went to the Floyd Road trail head because they have a bike rental shop. There is ample free parking and the ride is wooded providing shade from the sun. If you go south, you'll hit a covered bridge and a couple of other bridges that take you over the highway, which adds to the fun!

## Atlanta BeltLine: Trails

**Where:** Currently open 3.5 miles of trails around the city of Atlanta

**When:** Anytime

**Web:**   http://bit.ly/jTLKnZ

The Atlanta BeltLine, with help from the PATH Foundation, will connect Atlanta's in-town neighborhoods and could eventually connect to a broader path network for the entire metro area. The BeltLine is a great place to ride a bike, walk or even roller skate with playgrounds and parks along the way.

Currently there is 3.5 miles of trails completed, representing 10 percent of the total system at completion. The two segments open are the West End/Westview Trail in Southwest Atlanta which is approximately 2.5 miles in length and connects the neighborhoods of West End, Westview and Mozely Park. The other completed segment is the Northside Trail, in northwest Atlanta. It's approximately one mile long and goes through Tanyard Creek Park (which has two playgrounds), Louise G. Howard Park and Atlanta Memorial Park (has a playground), connecting the neighborhoods of Collier Hills and Collier Hills North. A third trail on the Eastside which is roughly 2.5 miles from 10th St. and Monroe Ave. to Dekalb Ave., connecting Piedmont Park to the Freedom Trail and Historic Fourth Ward is scheduled to open this summer.

For something a little extra, head to the nearly eight miles of interim hiking trails now open on the Eastside of the BeltLine and the Southwest. These segments are hosting the Art on the BeltLine project where local artists produce pieces displayed on the BeltLine trail.

# Nature Centers

## Autrey Mill Nature Preserve and Heritage Center

**Where:** 9770 Autrey Mill Rd., Johns Creek
(678-366-3511)

**When:** Grounds open 8 am – dusk,
Visitors Center Mon – Sat. 10 – 4 pm

**Web:** http://www.autreymill.org/

The Autrey Mill Nature Preserve and Heritage Center is 46 acres of forest and 2 miles of walking trails. There is a visitor's center with live animals including several different snakes. Heritage Village is an assembly of historic buildings from the mid-1800's including a landowner and tenant farmer house, plus an American Indian Teepee. The center also has a farm equipment museum that is open on select days. Autrey Mill hosts various events throughout the year including guided nature hikes. Check the website for the latest events.

# Noah's Ark Animal Rehabilitation Center

**Where:**     712 L G Griffin Rd., Locust Grove, Ga. (770-957-0888)

**When:**     Tues. – Sat. 12 – 3 pm

**Web:**      http://www.noahs-ark.org/

Noah's Ark is a center for injured, abused, and orphaned animals. They provide wildlife rehabilitation and when possible, release wildlife back into its natural habitat. Animals that can't make it on their own stay at the Center. Noah's Ark has more than 1,000 animals including exotic animals such as a black bear, tiger, and lion. Call beforehand to make sure the habitats are open.

# Dauset Trails

**Where:** 360 **Mt.Vernon** Rd., Jackson,GA
(770-775-6798)

**When:** Mon. -Sat. 9 – 5 pm, Sun. 12 – 5 pm

**Web:**  http://www.dausettrails.com/

Dauset Trails, about 40 minutes south of Atlanta, is a private, non-profit center and the dream of Hampton Daughtry and his childhood friend David Settle. The preserve includes 1200 acres of scenic trails, creeks, lakes, flora, and wildlife. In addition, there is a visitor's center, Animal Trail, Farm Trail, manicured gardens, and picnic area. They have designated hiking, biking trails and horse riding trails, but you have to bring your own bike or horse. Bring several quarters, too. Along the Animal Trail there are feeding stations and of course the animals interact more when you're feeding them. My boys were immediately taken in by the large bream in the pond. The turtles were a draw too, especially the impressive snapping turtle.

Across the pond is the Animal Trail. Here you can see rehabilitated cougars, raccoons, various birds of prey, a black bear, river otters, a beaver, and more. On the Farm Trail we saw goats, pigs, cows, chickens, and horses. In addition to the farm buildings, there is a blacksmith area and syrup making facilities. The Wonder Room is in the basement of the visitor's center and showcases, among other things, reptiles common in the area, as well as a classroom for groups.

We didn't have time to meander along the trails too much, but at the Visitor's Center you can pick up a "pleasure hunt" form that can be used on the Woodland Garden Trail. It lists 29 things to "find" on the trail. It looks like these are inanimate objects that have been placed in the garden, so it's an easy search and find rather than a nature identification activity. If nature identification is more your bag, head out to the Tree Trail with another sheet available at the Visitor's Center that asks you to match the numbered trees with the name of the tree. There are 31 different kinds of trees to identify.

Dauset Trails also has an extensive event calendar including outdoor movies and festivals.

# Dunwoody Nature Center

**Where:** 5343 Roberts Dr., Dunwoody, (770-394-3322)

**When:** Sun up to sundown seven days a week

**Web:** http://www.dunwoodynature.org/

Dunwoody Nature Center is an oasis in the suburbs. The Center features woodland, creekside and wetlands hiking, as well as a shaded playground and playhouse. There is an activity building which is the center for camps and classes. My boys were intrigued by the playhouse, but drawn to the creek. We all took our shoes off and waded, cooling off from the oppressive Georgia heat. My oldest even caught a tiny fish that flopped out of his hand and back to freedom.

The center offers plenty of structured programming, but it's also a great place for do-it-yourself discovery. In addition to take and return cards along the paths explaining plant and wildlife you may see, the center also offers I-Spy backpacks for a $10 fee. The backpacks include a parent guidebook with sample questions and activities for all ages from pre-school through high school. You'll also find field guides, drawing materials, story books, and games.

While you are there, be sure to find the bottle cap sculptures. Throughout the center you'll find a butterfly, frog, turtle, and more all made from bottle and other plastic caps. What a fun and creative way to recycle.

## Arabia Mountain Heritage Area

**Where:**  3787 Klondike Rd., Lithonia (770-484-3060)

**When:**  7 am - Sunset

**Web:**  http://www.arabiaalliance.org/

Arabia Mountain Heritage Area is located within a 20-minute drive east of the City of Atlanta and encompasses land in DeKalb, Rockdale and Henry County. The center of the heritage area is Davidson-Arabia Mountain Nature Preserve; a DeKalb County Park comprised of 2,000 acres of granite outcrop, wetlands, pine and oak forests, streams, and a lake. Ride bikes on the multi-use PATH trail through the woodland and past rock outcrops. There are also special events in the area, so check the website for the latest.

## Helpful Links:

**Piedmont Park Playgrounds:**
http://www.piedmontpark.org/do/playgrounds.html

**Piedmont Park Fishing:**
http://www.piedmontpark.org/do/fishing.html

**Piedmont Park Skating/Bike paths:**
http://www.piedmontpark.org/do/bikes.html

**Piedmont Park Dog Park:**
http://www.piedmontpark.org/do/dogpark.html

**Piedmont Park Green Market:**
http://bit.ly/lxjt3e

**Centennial Olympic Park Playgrounds**:
http://bit.ly/kC9kBh

**National Park Service, Georgia Parks:**
http://www.nps.gov/findapark/index.htm

**National Park Service, Augusta Canal and Heritage Center:**
http://bit.ly/meMA13

**National Park Service, Junior Ranger Program**:
http://www.nps.gov/learn/juniorranger.cfm

**National Park Service, WebRangers:**
http://www.webrangers.us/index.cfm

**Silver Comet Trail, Floyd Rd. Trail:**
http://bit.ly/ixWLJC

**Silver Comet Trail, Chief Ladiga Trail:**
http://bit.ly/iWUVfv

**Art on the BeltLine:**
http://bit.ly/ivymzS

**Dauset Trails Hiking and Biking Trails**:
http://www.dausettrails.com/trails.htm

**Dauset Trails Horse Trails:**
http://www.dausettrails.com/horse.htm

**Dunwoody Nature Center I-Spy Backpack**:
http://www.dausettrails.com/horse.htm

# ~ Sports ~

Every parent looks for ways to get their kids moving and burn some energy. There are lots of places in Atlanta that offer free classes for kids to try out a new sport, in addition to playing one they already know. Several of the professional sports teams in Atlanta, such as The Atlanta Braves and Atlanta Thrashers, offer opportunities for kids to interact with their favorite team.

# Atlanta Braves

## Atlanta Braves Birthday Present

**Where:** Turner Field

**Web:**  http://www.braves.com/birthday

**Cost:**  Birthday individual is free. Braves tickets start at $8

Celebrate your birthday at Turner Field with a present from the Atlanta Braves. Register online to receive a free companion admission to one game during the 2011 season to see the Atlanta Braves at Turner Field.

## Atlanta Braves Community Caravan

**Where:**          Across the Southeast

**When:**           Jan. – Feb. 2012

**Web:**            http://atmlb.com/iqkoJj

For the past few years, as a special thank you to fans, the Atlanta Braves hit the road in a caravan that brings the team and players to the fans. The caravan generally makes stops in Georgia Alabama,

North Carolina, South Carolina, and Tennessee before the team heads to Orlando for spring training.

Atlanta Braves players, coaches, alumni, broadcasters, and team executives make community appearances at children's hospitals, schools, and military bases, and host autograph signings. Go to the Braves website in December for information on exact locations.

## Thrashers Open Practices

**Where:** The Ice Forum
2300 Satellite Blvd
Duluth (770-813-1010)

**When:** Check the website for 2011
open practices

**Web:** http://bit.ly/iiKHmA

Atlanta Thrashers practice sessions are free and open to the public. For school age fans, the times probably don't mesh with your schedule, but for young fans, what a great opportunity to see your favorite hockey players up close. During the 2010-2011 season there were even a few Saturday practices. The 2011-2012 schedule isn't out yet, but check the Thrashers website for details closer to the season.

# Bowling

## Kids Bowl Free

**Where:**  Select Bowling Centers (Georgia includes Decatur, Brunswick, Stockbridge, Griffin & Thomasville)

**When:**  Check the registration page for the specific bowling alley and dates. Some start April 1 and some May 1. Program goes until Aug. 30 for some or as late as Oct. 31 in Stockbridge

**Web:**  http://www.kidsbowlfree.com/

**Cost:**  FREE (Add on up to 4 adults for only $24.95)

Students under 15 who register with the bowling alley (you need to register with each alley if you want to go to more than one) receive two free games per day. Shoe rental is extra, so if you bowl a lot, you may want to invest in bowling shoes.

For adults that want to join in the fun, there is a special Family Pass. For a $24.95 one-time fee, up to four adults can get the same two free games daily per person. That's a fabulous deal for the whole summer.

# Brunswick Zone Bowling

**Where:** Brunswick Lanes

**When:** Summer and Holidays

**Web:** http://bit.ly/luGaOS

Join Brunswick's Bonus Zone, include your child's birthday and receive free bowling coupons and discounts by email. Brunswick will email the coupons for free games to your inbox. Note this deal does not include shoe rental.

# 300 Atlanta Bowling

**What:** Kids Club Card

**Where:** 300 Atlanta, 2175 Savoy Dr., Atlanta (770-451-8605)

**When:** May 23 – Sept. 4

**Web:** http://www.threehundred.com/atlanta.html

At 300 Atlanta, kids 12 and under can pick up a 2011 Kids Club Card for free bowling. Cardholders receive one free game & shoe rental every day this summer. Must be 12 years or younger to qualify. The card is redeemable Sun-Fri before 5 pm.

## AMF Summer Unplugged

**Where:**          Participating AMF Bowling Centers

**When:**           June, July and August

**Web:**            http://freebowling.amf.com/

AMF's summer bowling program is called Summer Unplugged and offers free bowling for kids age 16 and under. Registration is required and began in April. In addition, adults with children registered for free bowling can purchase an AMF Summer 17 Plus Pass, good for up to four people ages 17 and older to bowl. Call your local AMF bowling center to make sure they are participating and get the details and restrictions for that center. This deal does not include shoe rental.

# Sports Lessons

## Learn to Play Water Polo

**Where:**          20 Willow Glenn Dr., Marietta, Ga.
                    No phone but here's an email:
                    krakenwapo@gmail.com

**When:**           Under 10 practice is Wed. from 10am – 11am.
                    Middle and high school groups are 8am – 12pm

**Web:**            http://krakenwaterpolo.webs.com/

**Cost:**           Trial Week is Free After that is a one-time fee. Contact
                    Kraken for 2011 fees.

If you are looking for something a little different for the kids to do this summer, try water polo!

Kraken Water Polo began in 2006 when a group of 14 high school swimmers got together for a friendly scrimmage.  Now the group has several teams of differing age levels and offers instruction for new players. Best news, you can try it out for free.

Middle and high school aged kids are invited to practice with the team for a week free to determine if they want to play. For specific instruction times, contact Kraken via email. Instruction is broken into water and land practice. All swimming abilities are welcome and each week there is an official game.

Children 10 and under and invited too. They practice once a week on Wed. mornings from 10 – 11 and learn basic skills, rules and general fitness.

For more information on the youth practices, contact Owen Sweitzer at owen.sweitzer@gmail.com.

# Kids Golf Free at Stone Mountain Golf Club

**Where:**   Marriott Golf Clubs
(including Stone Mountain Golf Club)
1145 Stonewall Jackson Dr., St. Mtn. (770-465-3278)

**When:**   Anytime after 3pm with a paying adult 365 days a year

**Web:**   http://bit.ly/mmR0hv

**Cost:**   Free for kids when accompanied by a paying adult

Designed to promote the game of golf among young people, Kids Golf-4-Free allows kids 15 years old and under to play for free after 3:00 p.m., when accompanied by a full paying adult.

In addition, Kids Rent-4-Free provides junior golfers participating in Kids Golf-4-Free with a free rental set of Accu-Length clubs for use during their round.

Available at select Marriott Golf properties, Kids Golf-4-Free also enables kids to receive a free golf lesson when accompanied by an adult who is taking a fully paid golf lesson from a Marriott Golf instructor.

All of these programs are based on availability and restrictions may apply, so contact the Stone Mountain Golf Club to reserve your tee time or lesson and ask about the program.

# Tennis Lessons at Bitsy Grant Tennis Center Family Festival

**Where:** Bitsy Grant Tennis Center
2125 Northside Dr., Atlanta
(404-609-7193)

**When:** Sat. and Sun., Aug. 6-7, 2011

**Web:** http://bit.ly/k9r7zh

The Bitsy Grant Tennis Center in Buckhead is hosting a Family Fun Festival to coincide with the Georgia State Adult/Senior Open Tennis Championship in August 2011. In addition to the Championship, kids' activities include a moonwalk and free tennis lessons through the United States Tennis Associations' Quick Start program for kids ages 5 – 10. For more information contact Peter Howell, at 678-644-9263 or www.bitsytennis.com

# Biking lessons at The Dick Lane Velodrome

**Where:** The Dick Lane Velodrome
1889 Lexington Ave., East Point
(770-813-4930)

**When:** Every Monday and Thursday, Mar. – Oct. (weather permitting)
5:30 – 6:30 pm for kids 8 – 12
6:30 – 7:30 pm for kids 13-16

**Web:** http://bit.ly/lzvQFy

**Cost:** Free for East Point Residents (others are asked to make a once yearly donation of $50 if family budgets allow)

The Dick Lane Velodrome in East Point allows kids to ride around the big Velodrome track and they offer a free Bicycle Little League program for kids ages 8-16 years old to show them how to do it safely.

The program is coached by experienced bicycle riders and racers and shows children how to safely operate their bikes on the banked track. Once they get comfortable, they'll have the opportunity to compete under the close supervision of the coaches and under the lights during Pro Race Series events.

Classes aren't held when it's raining, so check the weather page before going out. Bikes and helmets are provided, so you don't need to haul a bike with you. However, participants must bring a parent-signed waiver. There are no reservations, just show up. For more information contact Jeff Hopkins, jeff@dicklanevelodrome.com.

# Football Clinic with NFL Pros

| **Where:** | James Hallford Stadium<br>3789 Memorial College Ave.<br>(410-850-5900) |
|---|---|
| **When:** | Saturday, June 11, 2011, 10 am – 2 pm<br>(pre-registration required) |
| **Web:** | http://bit.ly/kq4hNb |

Atlanta Falcons Chauncey Davis and Jonathan Babineaux, along with Atlanta native and former Baltimore Raven Daniel Wilcox, are headlining a free one-day football camp for middle and high schoolers grades 7 – 12. In addition to football drills, students will learn about fitness and nutrition from professional trainer Rich Garcia, receive SAT/ACT preparation from Bell Curves, and hear all about the recruiting process.

After lunch, parents and students will receive an overview of the college recruiting process by a representative from the National Collegiate Scouting Association (NCSA) and have an opportunity to engage Davis, Babineaux, and Wilcox during a question and answer session. Register online by June 9!

# All-Comers Track and Field Meets

**Where:**        Emory University's Woodruff Physical Education Center, 26 Eagle Row, Atlanta (404-727-6551)

**When:**         Tuesdays May 3 – June 14, 2011. Gates open at 5:00 and events start at 5:30 pm

**Web:**          http://www.atlantatrackclub.org/

**Cost:**         Spectators are free. $1 for Youth/Student Athletes, $2 for Adult Athletes

Each Tuesday for seven weeks, the Atlanta Track Club sponsors All-Comers meets at Emory University. Come to one meet or try all of them! Events include running races, throwing the shot put, long jump and high jump. The events are for all ages and there are different brackets for different age groups from children under 6 to adults. The schedule is an estimate and sometimes races start a bit early on days when attendance is light, so come early.

# BMX Tracks

**Where:**        Noonday Park, 489 Hawkins Store Rd., NE Kennesaw (770-591-3160)

Wild Horse, Powder Springs, 4070 Macedonia Rd. Powder Springs (770-943-5493)

**When:**         Whenever they don't have a BMX bike event

**Web:**          http://prca.cobbcountyga.gov/BMX.htm

Noonday Park in Kennesaw and Wild Horse in Powder Springs are public parks with BMX tracks that when not in use for races, practice or maintenance, are free to ride – just bring your bike and a helmet. We've even hosted birthday parties at the track. The best part is the kids (even the older kids) LOVE it. It's challenging enough for someone who rides, as the trick becomes to get more air when you jump, but easy enough that anyone can make it around the track. Before you go, know that BMX of Cobb County runs the park and has the right of first refusal. This means that if they are having a race, or doing maintenance work on the track, you won't be able to get on it.

Check their website to see when they have races. The day before they may have trials, too, so if you are planning an event at the park, it would be best to call beforehand.

## University of Georgia G-Day

**Where:** Sanford Stadium, Athens

**When:** Saturday in April

**Web:** http://bit.ly/lSxorC
(this is the 2011 site URL, it may not work for 2012, if not, try http://www.georgiadogs.com)

If you've never been to a University of Georgia football game between the hedges, it's an experience. This family friendly scrimmage is a great opportunity for Dawg fans (and football fans) to see some spring football. The annual G-Day spring football game in Athens features the Bulldog team split into the Red and Black squads.

# Public Swimming Pools

## Free Swimming: Piedmont Park Pool

**Where:** Piedmont Park Pool, Piedmont Park
1071 Piedmont Ave, Atlanta
404. 875.7275 x324

**When:** Free hours are Mon.-Fri. 3 – 5 pm

**Other Times:** $4 per adult; $2 for 16 and under or over 55;
$1 for 5 and under

**Web:** http://bit.ly/jvrKyw

The beautiful Piedmont Park pool will celebrate its third season this summer. This state of the art pool has separate lap lanes, fountains, zero entry, stairs, wheelchair entry, lazy river, whirlpool and lots of various elevations, great for children of all sizes. I especially liked the "seats" in the water around the pool. In addition to being a great place for adults to sit in the water, it's perfect for little ones who want to splash around, while older siblings swim in the deeper water. There is one small corner that is 6 ft. deep, but for the most part, it's not over 4 ft. deep.

My boys LOVED the lazy river and the whirlpool. Judging from the crowds there, they weren't the only ones! This pool is VERY popular and can get quite crowded. The day we went it was a bit too crowded for me. However, my boys really had fun, adding it was a great place for tag, lots of places to hide, and nooks and crannies to get away.

Although we didn't use it, there is also a refreshment stand, so if you forgot to pack lunch or the kids get the munchies (mine are always STARVING at the pool) this is a great option. Right outside the gate is a playground surrounded by walking/biking/skating paths. If the weather is dicey, check the website to find out if any of the areas of the pool are closed before you go.

# Free Swimming: Garden Hills Pool

**Where:** 335 Pine Tree Dr. NE
Atlanta (404-848-7220)

**When:** Open 10:30 – 8:30 pm
After 5 pm members only

**Web:** http://gardenhillspool.com/

**Cost:** Free hours: Mon. – Fri.
10:30 – 12:30 pm

**Other times:**   $4 per adult; $2 for 16 and
under or over 55; $1 for 5
and under 5

The Garden Hills pool offers a deep end and diving board, as well as lap lanes and shallow area. It also has a kiddie pool and a snack bar. Garden Hills pool is situated between a shady playground and a large playing field, perfect to keep the little ones busy during adult swim.

## Free Swimming: Chastain Park Pool

| | |
|---|---|
| **Where:** | 235 W. Wieuca Rd., Atlanta, (404-841-9196) |
| **When:** | Open 10 – 8 pm After 5 pm members only |
| **Web:** | http://www.chastainparkathleticclub.org/page1.aspx |
| **Cost:** | Free hours: Mon. – Fri. 10 – 12:30 pm |
| **Other times:** | $4 per adult; $2 16 and under or over 55; $1 5 and under 5 |

Chastain Park pool is a less crowded alternative to the Piedmont Park pool. Although Piedmont has some cool features like a lazy river and whirlpool, Chastain Park has essentially three pools:  a deep pool, lap pool, and shallow end. The deep pool has a diving board on one side and on the other side is a swimming area, perfect for playing sharks and minnows. The lap pool has starting blocks and lanes and the shallow pool is a maximum of 3' 6" in depth and has stairs across one entire end, perfect for the little guys.

There are lots of shady places to camp out and a snack bar for refreshments. Tables next to the snack bar are a perfect place for a picnic lunch. The day we went it was cool. I thought this might affect the crowds, so I asked the lifeguard if normally it was more crowded. He said the weekends, especially Sunday, are busy, but normal days are not too crowded.

# Free Swimming: Grant Park Pool

| | |
|---|---|
| **Where:** | 625 Park Avenue SE, Atlanta, (404-622-3041) |
| **When:** | Varies, see site for day and times |
| **Web:** | http://www.grantparkpool.org/contact.html |
| **Cost:** | Free hours: Mon. – Fri. 1:30 – 4:00 pm |
| **Other times:** | $4 per adult; $2 16 and under or over 55; $1 5 and under 5 |

The Grant Park pool underwent a total transformation in 2008. Little kids can splash right into the new zero entry pool, which gradually slopes downward like a beach. The new splash spot spouts water from various points, while the big blue awning provides much needed shade. The bathhouse has been completely renovated, as has the large pool. * Note: This is 2010 information. Visit the website or call before heading to the pool.

# Spray Fountains

## Centennial Olympic Park Fountain of Rings, Water Show & Playgrounds

**Where:** Centennial Olympic Park, 265 Park Ave. West NW
Atlanta (404-223-4499)

**When:** Splash around anytime. Daily Shows are 12:30, 3:30, 6:30 and 9 pm

**Web:** http://bit.ly/iFxJgv

The Fountain of Rings is the centerpiece of Centennial Olympic Park and is one of the most recognized and photographed landmarks in Georgia. When you go, be sure to take a towel and change of clothes because no one can resist jumping from ring to ring between the shooting water spouts.

Take a break from splashing during select times and watch the light and water show which includes music such as the 1812 Overture and Under the Sea. Shows are daily at 12:30, 3:30, 6:30 and 9 pm.

In addition to the Fountains, there is a wide open area perfect for football or Frisbee. There are also two playgrounds. One is specifically designed for all children, including those with physical disabilities.

## More Fountains

Thanks to Jenni from Forsyth for Families (http://bit.ly/m30y2R) we have several fountains to add to our list. Most of these are free, but there is one I included because at $1, it's so inexpensive. Here's what Jenni has to say about the various fountains: Pack a picnic, swimsuit, and a change of clothes and off you go! Playtown is a shady playground and the town center has lots of space for picnics as well as shops and restaurants. Duluth Town Green has shady areas, benches and swings, a playground and surrounding shops and restaurants that make it inviting for an afternoon. For extras such as art shows and concerts please check websites for calendar of events

## Mall of Georgia Fountains

**Where:**     Mall of Georgia, 3333 Buford Dr.
            Buford (770-271-9458)

**Web:**       http://bit.ly/jozCyM

## Suwanee Town Center Park Fountains and Playtown

**Where:**     Suwanee Town Center Park, 330 Town Center Ave.
            Suwanee (770-945-2792)

**Web:**       http://bit.ly/jo4pvw

# Duluth Town Green Fountains

**What:** Splash Fountains

**Where:** Duluth Town Green
         3578 West Lawrenceville St.
         Duluth (770-476-3434)

**Web:** http://bit.ly/ltsOTF

# Spraygrounds in Roswell: Riverside Park

**Where:**      Riverside Park, 575 Riverside Rd.
             Roswell (770-594-6158)

**When:**       10 – 7 pm, closed on Tuesdays

**Web:**        http://bit.ly/meUFaU

**Cost:**       $1 for 1 year old and up, Adults are free if you're just
             watching, $1 if you splash around with the kids

# Spraygrounds in Roswell: E. Roswell Park

**Where:**      East Roswell Park, 9000 Fouts Rd.
             Roswell (770-594-6188)

**When:**       10 – 7 pm, closed on Wednesdays

**Web:**        http://bit.ly/meUFaU

**Cost:**       $1 for 1 year old and up, Adults are free if you're just
             watching, $1 if you jump in with the kids

# Dancing: CORE's Lunchtime in the Studio

**Where:** Core Performance Studio
         133 Sycamore St.
         Decatur (404-373-4154)

**When:** Generally Select Thursdays 12 – 1 pm

**Web:**   http://bit.ly/kFEmCM

Lunchtime in the Studio showcases the creation and performance of dance by CORE Performance Company in an informal setting – and the audience even gets free lunch! The series of five lunchtime performances are free and open to the public. It's a wonderful opportunity to see dancers up close. The performances are held from late September through May. 2011 dates have not been set, but watch their website for the announcement. Generally, they choose Thursdays and the sessions will always be between 12 and 1pm. The event takes place at CORE Studios at 139 Sycamore St. on the Square in Downtown Decatur. Although this is not strictly a kid-centered event, I imagine any child would love to see dancers up close and watch how the company creates the dances.

## Helpful Links

**Stone Mountain Golf:**
http://bit.ly/igZtSQ

**Cobb County BMX:**
http://bit.ly/mQLXxV

# ~Miscellaneous Fun~

Check out this interesting assortment of one-of-a-kind activities! Remember, free days and programs change without notice, so always call before you go to make sure the event or program is still running.

## Mayfield Dairy

**Where:** 1160 Broadway Ave., Braselton (888-298-0396)

**When:** Mon. – Fri., 10 - 4 pm, Sat., 10 - 1 pm, No tours on Wednesday

**Web:** http://www.mayfielddairy.com/

**Cost:** Free, but you'll spend about $2 – $3 for an ice cream cone afterwards

Mayfield Dairy is a quick stop off I-85 from Atlanta toward Charlotte, NC. The Braselton factory is where they make Mayfield milk (the ice cream is made in Athens, TN). The tour starts with a short video, which was more like a long commercial for Mayfield. After the movie, don hairnets and go into the plant. You'll see large machines that process the milk, including the Aro-Vac. When cows eat onions or other strong foods, it can change the way the milk tastes. The Aro-Vac uses heat and steam to vaporize and remove unwanted flavors and odors from the milk. You'll also see the trucks that bring the milk in (24 hours a day) and watch them fill the bottles. It was an interesting tour, especially for a bunch of city kids who think milk comes from Publix.

# Krispy Kreme Donuts

**Where:** 295 Ponce De Leon Ave., Atlanta (404-876-7307)

**When:** Anytime

**Web:** http://www.krispykreme.com/home

**Cost:** Free to watch them make donuts, glazed donuts are $.99, a dozen for $6.99. The hot chocolate is pretty good, too, and costs $1.99

When the sign light is on, the donuts are hot! If you've ever wondered how donuts are made, the Krispy Kreme store on Ponce de Leon lets you watch donuts as they go through the assembly line process. Kids can see how the donuts rise, then are flipped as they fry. My favorite part is watching them travel through the white waterfall of sugary goodness that gives them the wonderful "krispyness". There are few things better than a piping hot Krispy Kreme glazed donut right off the line. Don't forget the free souvenir Krispy Kreme hat!

# Dragon Con Parade

**Where:** Downtown Atlanta

**When:** Sept. 3, 2011 10 am

**Web:** http://www.dragoncon.org/events.php
http://bit.ly/lBbHlU

This parade is a MUST do. Like the Peachtree Road Race, if you're going to live in Atlanta, you need to do this at least once. If you don't live in Atlanta, this is definitely worth the trip.

The annual Dragon Con convention in downtown Atlanta is the premier sci-fi convention that showcases everything sci-fi – Klingons, Stormtroppers, pirates, Quiddich players, Mad Max, Ghostbusters, superheroes, and more. Although you need a ticket for the convention, you don't need a thing to watch the amazingly bizarre parade of convention participants that takes place on Saturday morning. Plan to stay for lunch and you could end up sitting next to a Wookiee! This parade gets more exposure and more crowded each year, so be sure to get there early and bring an extra dose of patience.

The parade begins promptly at 10 am. The route goes from Woodruff Park (at Peachtree St. and Auburn Ave.) north on Peachtree St. back to the Hyatt's front entrance, then onto Baker St., and finally to the Marriott's front entrance on Peachtree Center Ave. where the parade ends. Previous events have had more than 1400 costumed members of Dragon Con strutting their stuff down Peachtree and spilling out onto the sidewalks, too. Be warned, some of these costumes are VERY good, and participants are encouraged to interact with the crowd, so your little ones could get scared.

However, if you have a crew like mine that have been entertained by Percy Jackson and Camp Half-Blood or can name all the planets, ships, and characters in Star Wars in alphabetical order forwards and backwards, this field trip is a winner.

## Silver Scream Spookshow

**Where:** Plaza Theatre, 1049 Ponce De Leon Ave. NE, Atlanta (404)873-1939

**When:** The last Saturday of every month at 1 pm

**Web:** http://www.silverscreamspookshow.com/

**Cost:** Kids 12 and Under are free, Over 12 and Adults $7

Before showing a vintage horror film, the Silver Scream Spookshow begins with a half hour variety show featuring Professor Mortes and his side-kick Retch. The Spookshow is a cross between "Pee Wee Herman's Playhouse" and "The Munsters" and features magic tricks, dance numbers, and a little spooking. It's as low budget as the films screened afterwards, but it has an endearing, cult-like feel that makes it a must see for anyone looking for something a little off beat. "Characters" greet you as you walk in and are available for photos after the show.

# Summer Movies

I love watching outdoor movies in the summer. There is a great line-up this summer of places offering free summer flicks. Here is a list of places available at press time and a few you might want to check again in June. Thanks to Paul at Southern Outdoor Cinema for helping gather this information.

## Georgia Movies in the Park (TM)

**Where:** Dunwoody, Dawsonville, Johns Creek, Canton and Cumming

**When:** **Johns Creek** - June 11 (Gulliver's Travels), July 9 & August 13

**Cumming** - July 16 & Fall (Sponsored by Girls on the Run)

**Canton** - TBA

**Dunwoody** - TBA

**Dawsonville** - June 3 (Movie on Lake Lanier) & August 19

**Web:** www.GaMoviesInThePark.com
www.facebook.com/SouthernOutdoorCinema

Georgia Movies in the Park is Georgia's longest running "festival and outdoor movie event". It returns to North Georgia for another summer of free wholesome outdoor movies the entire family can enjoy. Each event begins with festival activities including a bounce house, children's activities, face painters and vendors. Blockbuster films are shown in High Definition (HD) on a cinematic-quality Airscreen movie screen. Sponsored by Southern Outdoor Cinema LLC, City of Johns Creek and Dawson County Parks & Recreation.

# Summer Screen on the Green Movie Series @ The Avenue Webb Gin

**Where:** The Avenue Webb Gin

**When:** From 6:30 – 8:30 pm

June 4, June 18, July 9, July 23, August 6

**Web:** www.shoptheavenue.com
www.facebook.com/shoptheavenue

Complimentary children's activities including bounce house, face painting, and balloon art. Food and drink available for purchase.

# Summer Screen on the Green Movie Series @ The Avenue Peachtree City

**Where:** The Avenue Peachtree City
239 City Circle, Peachtree City, GA 30269

**When:** 6 pm for activities,

**Movies begin at sundown:** June 10, June 24, July 8 & July 22

**Web:** www.peachtreecity.shoptheavenue.com/

Complimentary children's activities including bounce house and face painting. Popcorn available for purchase.

# Sweet Apple Village Family Movie Nights

**Where:** Sweet Apple Village
12070 Etris Road, Roswell, GA 30075

**When:** Held on the 4th Thursday of the month while school is out and the 4th Saturday in September.

Thursday, June 23rd - Diary of a Wimpy Kid 2

Thursday, July 28th - Rio

Saturday, September 24th - TBD

Saturday, August 27th - TBD - Just for Mom and Dad
Date Night/Girl's Night Out Movie

**Web:**          www.sweetapplevillage.com.
                  Join the e-Village to receive event reminders and updates.

These are family friendly nights of fun and free outdoor viewing of pre-home release films. Also, check their website for details on pre-movie night book clubs and activities for kids in months showing book adaptation films.

## Summer Movies Under the Stars in Dahlonega

**Where:**        Hancock Park, Dahlonega
                  Located just off of the square at the corner of North Park
                  Street and Warwick Street.

**When:**         June 10, July 8, August 12

**Web:**          www.dahlonega.org or
                  Dahlonega Chamber of Commerce at 706-864-3711

## Outdoor Movies at the Depot – Gainesville

**Where:**        The Gainesville Arts Council
                  331 Spring St, SW, Gainesville GA

**When:**         June 9th & August 4

**Web:**          http://www.theartscouncil.net/

## Cinema on the Green

**Where:**        On the square in downtown McDonough, GA

**When:**         July 30 – TBD, October 29 - TBD

**Web:**          http://bit.ly/mj8kox

## Popcorn in the Park - Snellville

**Where:**        2342 Oak Road, Snellville GA

**When:**         June 11th, July 16th from 6-10:30 PM.

**Web:**          http://www.snellvillepride.com/

# Friday Night Flicks  - Clarksville

**Where:**        Pitts Park, 458 Jefferson Street, Clarkesville, GA 30523
              706-754-2220

**When:**         June 3, July 8, August 12

**Other Movie Opportunities that were not available at press time include:**

### Atlantic Station Outdoor Movies on the Green

**Web:**              www.atlanticstation.com

### East Cobb Park Outdoor Movies

**Web:**              http://www.eastcobbpark.org/

### Flicks on 5th

**Web:**              http://bit.ly/jkeffF

This series has films that are geared toward college students, so they are usually PG-13 or R

# Georgia Tech: Kids@Kollege

**When:** Spring 2012
(Check website in January for exact date)

**Where:** Georgia Tech Campus – Outdoor fields
at the Campus Recreation Center

**Web:** http://georgiatechkids.com

**Cost:** Free, but pre-registration required.

Kids@Kollege is a fun annual event put on by the students and faculty of the Georgia Institute of Technology to bring elementary-school-aged kids (5-12 years old) onto the school's campus for a day of interactive science and cultural presentations, as well as recreational activities. It's also a way to spark their interest and excitement in pursuing a college education.

# Jugglers Festival

**Where:** Yaarab Shrine Center Recreation Bldg.
400 Ponce de Leon Ave., Atlanta, Ga.

**When:** Feb. 3 – 5, 2012 (check website for times)

**Web:** http://www.atlantajugglers.org/festival.htm

Each year in early February, the annual Groundhog Day Juggler's Festival is held at the Yaarab Shrine Center. The 3-day extravaganza features jugglers from all over the Southeast. Saturday is the day to come for juggling shows. Be there early so you don't miss the opening festivities that include the comical and joyous Seed and Feed Marching Abominable Band, one of my favorites.

# Helpful Links:

**Silver Scream Spookshow on GPB:**
http://bit.ly/lAJazN

# ~ Seasonal Events ~

Holidays for kids are a big deal. They love the activities and tradi-tions that go along with the season, whether that's trick or treating or singing holiday carols. Here's a list of free activities to do for vari-ous seasons. Since many of these activities or dates are not set in stone yet, make sure to visit the website or call the location before heading out to confirm the event details.

## Parade: Little Five Points Halloween Parade

**Where:** Down Euclid and Moreland Ave.
Little Five Points

**When:** Saturday in October
(see website for official date and time)

**Web:** http://www.l5phalloween.com/parade.htm

The Little Five Points (L5P) Halloween Parade is an off-beat adven-ture to get you in the mood for All Hallows Eve. This is one of those quirky local events that make Atlanta so much fun. My favorite is the Krewe of the Grateful Gluttons, a troupe of giant skeleton pup-pets. The Krewe hosts a skeleton building workshop each year and also publishes an online how-to guide, so now you have a Hallow-een project, too. The parade itself isn't overly scary, but there can be some gruesome and more adult oriented floats. To view past pa-rades, visit the Little Five Points Parade website.  After the parade, take a little time to browse around the funky shops in this area or have your picture taken in front of the giant skull (aka Vortex Bar and Grill). Vortex burgers are a wonderful thing, but unfortunately, the restaurant has gone to an adult only policy, so children 18 and under are not allowed in the restaurant. Instead, take them to Zesto and save room for a nut brown ice cream cone, my favorite.

# Christmas in Atlanta

## Parade: Children's Healthcare of Atlanta Christmas Parade

| | |
|---|---|
| **Where:** | Downtown Atlanta |
| **When:** | Sat., Dec. 3, 2011, 10:30 to 12 noon |
| **Web:** | http://www.choa.org/parade |
| **Cost:** | Free. bleacher seats available for purchase |

The Children's Healthcare of Atlanta Christmas parade is the largest Christmas parade in the Southeast and a great way to kick-start the holiday season. This is a popular parade, so get there a little early to get a good spot along the parade route, which follows Peachtree Street, turns right onto Marietta and finally turns left and ends on Centennial Olympic Park Drive. We generally try to find a spot near the beginning of the route, or even as far down as Ellis St. If you'd prefer to have a seat waiting, purchase a bleacher seat for $12. Any unclaimed bleacher seats are released to the public at 10:15 am, so if you don't get around to purchasing them beforehand, you can try the day of the event.

## Christmas in Atlanta: Larry, Carols & Mo

| | |
|---|---|
| **Where:** | The Fox Theatre, 660 Peachtree St. NE Atlanta (404-881-2100) |
| **When:** | 2011 date not set, but normally in early Dec. (check website for updated information) |
| | 6 pm doors open, 7 pm Holiday Sing-Along begins |
| **Web:** | http://www.foxtheatre.org/LarryCarolsMo.aspx |

Larry, Carols & Mo is becoming a tradition in Atlanta. The Fox Theatre is a site to behold for any event, but especially when it's free. The evening starts with an Organ Concert by the Fox Theatre's organist in residence Larry-Douglas Embury playing Mighty Mo, the Fox Theatre organ. Each year the sing-along features local musicians who are great about encouraging you to join in even if you can't sing. Afterwards they'll screen a movie (the 2010 feature was "Elf") and offer photos with Santa. Each year the Fox accepts donations for a good cause such as Toys for Tots or the Atlanta Food Bank.

Although this is a free event, you do need a reserved ticket. Tickets generally become available in early November and you need to get them right away or they'll be gone. Tickets are available at the Fox Theatre Box Office or Ticketmaster (although Ticketmaster fees apply).

# Christmas in Atlanta: Holiday Lights

One of the things I love about the holidays are the lights. There are numerous places in Atlanta with fantastic light displays you can view for a fee. Here are several places you can see lights for free.

## Holiday Lights: Centennial Olympic Park

**Where:** 265 Park Ave. West NW
Atlanta (404-222-7275)

**When:** Nov. – Jan. 2011
(see website for exact dates and times)

**Web:** http://bit.ly/IMCEFM

Different and unique every year, Holiday in Lights runs through the first week of January. The Park is open daily to view the lights from 7am to 11pm, including Christmas Day. The Holiday in Lights spirit is carried throughout the Georgia World Congress Center Authority campus, which includes the Georgia World Congress Center, the Georgia Dome, and Centennial Olympic Park. While you're there, save some time to go ice skating.

# Holiday Lights: Atlantic Station

**Where:**        1380 Atlantic Drive, Atlanta (404-733-1221)

**When:**        Nov. – Dec., 2011 (see website for exact dates and times)

**Web:**         http://www.atlanticstation.com/events.php

View 250,000 lights within an eight block radius. Gather around Atlantic Station's grand 50-foot tall Christmas Tree and experience the magic of a realistic snowfall during nightly shows (Snow is weather permitting and at specific times)

# Holiday Lights: Forsyth County Christmas Light Show

**Where:**        Bryn Ridge Ct, Cumming (in the Haley Farms Subdivision)

**When:**        Nov.– Jan. 2011

**Cost:**         Donations to benefit Family Haven

**Web:**         http://bit.ly/mklK7f

# Holiday Lights: The Village Green, Smyrna

**Where:**        200 Village Green Circle, Smyrna (770-431-2842)

**When:**        Dec – Jan., 2011 (see website for exact dates and times)

**Web:**         http://bit.ly/lJ0gtC

The Village Green area around the library, the Community Center, and the Veterans Memorial, along with the Market Village,–are all dressed in lights and holiday cheer through New Year's Eve/Day.

# Christmas in Atlanta: Live Nativities

Another favorite holiday tradition in our family is visiting one or more of the live nativity productions at local churches. Several are quite elaborate. Most churches do not have the specific dates available for the 2011 holiday season, so check their websites in November for specific dates or call the church. Many times the church websites are not updated in a timely manner, so you may want to call. Generally, the live nativities start in early December, so if you wait until the week before Christmas, chances are most will already have happened. All of these functions are free, but they do accept donations. Don't forget to wear warm clothes, as most of the activities are held outside.

# Live Nativities:
## Roswell United Methodist Church

**Where:** Roswell United Methodist Church
814 Mimosa Blvd.
Roswell (770-993-6218)

**When:** Early December
(contact the church for exact dates and times)

**Web:** http://www.rumc.com/bethlehem

Roam through a 1st century marketplace, brought to life by costumed characters and real, stable animals. Share the excitement of shepherds, Roman soldiers, shopkeepers, and artisans, and witness the live production that tells the story of the very first Christmas.

# Live Nativities:
## St. John's United Methodist Church

**Where:** St. John's United Methodist Church
550 Mount Paran Rd., NW
Sandy Springs (404-255-1384)

**When:** Early December
(contact the church for exact dates and times)

**Web:** http://bit.ly/kARhZa

We go to this live nativity every year and it's quite elaborate. Take a walking journey along a torch lighted path to the ancient city of Bethlehem. Be prepared to "make your mark" for the census in order to enter the city gates, guarded by Roman soldiers. Inside is a bustling street, lined with stalls full of bread, drinks, and herbs for sale. Watch as a blacksmith finishes refining a sword for a soldier, or listen as school children learn Hebrew and recite stories. A fortune teller picks stones and holds them to the light to tell the future. There is a place to hitch the camels before entering the palace of King Herod, which is guarded by more soldiers. The sound of angels singing brings guests outside the city. Out of the hustle and bustle, there is a barn with Mary, Joseph, and the baby Jesus. The couple's donkey is hitched close by and the three kings wait patiently for their cue to bring the gifts.

# Live Nativities: Sardis United Methodist Church

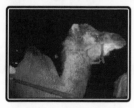

**Where:** Sardis United Methodist Church
3725 Powers Ferry Rd., NW
Atlanta (404-237-6060)

**When:** Early December

**Web:** http://sardischurch.com/index.php

This is a great, laid back production complete with camels, goats, and a furry bunny. There are straw seats in front of the stable and after the production, you can pet the animals then go into the beautiful and historic 1812 church for homemade cookies and hot cider.

# Live Nativities: Peachtree Lutheran Church

**Where:** Peachtree Lutheran Church
3686 Peachtree Rd., NE
Atlanta (404-233-7031)

**When:** Mid-December
(contact the church for exact dates and times)

**Web:** http://www.peachtreelutheran.org/

In addition to the normal cast, see live goats, sheep, donkeys and doves. I couldn't find anything about this on their website, so call before you go.

# Live Nativities:
# Snellville United Methodist Church

**Where:**     Snellville United Methodist Church
                2428 Main Street East
                Snellville, GA (770-972-9360)

**When:**      Mid-December
                (contact the church for exact dates and times)

**Web:**       http://bit.ly/lX6bBb

Take a journey to Bethlehem accompanied by a family traveling to pay their taxes. Along the way, they'll tell you the story of the birth of the Christ child. As you go, take part in an ancient marketplace where merchants peddle their wares (including live chickens), and storytellers pass down traditions. Try your hand at dipping candles, making dolls, or sample wares from local merchants. Witness Mary and Joseph traveling by donkey, Roman soldiers, the no-vacancy signs on all the inns, shepherds, sheep, goats, angels, Wise men traveling by camel (there is a live camel along with the other animals) and even a tax collector.

# Live Nativities:
# Chamblee First United Methodist Church

**Where:**     Chamblee First United Methodist Church
                4147 Chamblee Dunwoody Rd.
                Chamblee (770) 457-2525

**When:**      Early December
                (contact the church for exact dates and times)

**Web:**       http://www.chambleeumc.org/events/index.html

The Live Nativity is on the hill at the activities building behind the church. Children are allowed to pet the animals before and after the presentation, and the actors wear biblical costumes. A carol choir sings all of the familiar tunes as the story unfolds through music and narration. All are welcomed to cookies and hot chocolate in the Fellowship Hall following the drama.

# Live Nativities:
# Rock Spring Presbyterian Church

**Where:** Rock Spring Presbyterian Church
1824 Piedmont Ave.
Atlanta (404-875-7483)

**When:** Dec. 22 – 24
(contact the church for exact dates and times)

**Web:** http://www.rspc.org/activities.htm

Since 1954, the Live Nativity Scene has been held each evening from December 22 to 24 in front of the church as Rock Spring Presbyterian's tradition of celebrating the birth of Christ with the community.

# Christmas at the Governor's Mansion

**Where:** Governor's Mansion
391 West Paces Ferry Rd., NW
Atlanta (404-261-1776)

**When:** Two weeks in December
(check site or call for exact dates and times)

**Web:** http://bit.ly/iLndA0

Each December for two weeks, the Governor's Mansion is opened for tours of the decorated home. The dates vary from year-to-year, so check the website or give them a call to plan your trip. The program kicks off with a tree lighting ceremony that is open to the public. After the ceremony, guests are invited for a tour. In addition to the beautifully decorated Mansion, there are local choral groups that perform and children are served cider and cookies.

# St. Patrick's Day

## Parades: St. Patrick's Day

**Where:** Downtown Atlanta, Parade Route goes down Peachtree to Underground Atlanta

**When:** Saturday, March 17, 2012 at 12 noon

**Web:** http://www.stpatsparadeatlanta.com/

The best place to celebrate St. Patrick's Day is at the Atlanta's St. Patrick's Day Parade, which should be ultra fun in 2012 as St. Patrick's Day is on a Saturday. The parade begins at Peachtree St. and Ralph McGill and goes past Woodruff Park to Underground Atlanta.

If you like parades, and I do, this is a good one. Of course, there are the requisite marching bands, clowns, and schools of Irish dance with girls in those fabulous dresses, but this parade also has the 501st Stormtroopers from Star Wars, in kilts!

After the parade, head to Underground Atlanta for the St. Patrick's Day party and celebration. It's a family event with Irish dancers, singers and performers.

# Easter in Georgia

## Easter Egg Hunt at the Governor's Mansion

**Where:** Governor's Mansion
391 West Paces Ferry Rd., NW
Atlanta (404-261-1776)

**When:** Generally a week or two before Easter

**Web:** http://bit.ly/kbtAD5

**Contact:** (404) 261-1776 or
MansionEvents@georgia.gov
for more details

For the past nine years, the first lady of Georgia has hosted an Annual Easter Egg Hunt at the Georgia Governor's Mansion. Everyone is invited, but reservations are required and generally sell out fast, so you'll want to mark your calendar for the first day they take them (generally about 2 weeks before the event). In addition to an egg hunt, there are Easter themed games and activities for kids. The 2011 event included Easter Bunny Photos, a Moonwalk, Cupcake Decorating Station, Face Painting, a Storybook Station with books provided by Peachtree Publishers, an Easter Egg Roll, and an Easter Egg Decorating Station. The event is free, but each year participants are asked to make a donation for a specific charity. In 2011, they asked for new or unused stuffed animals and teddy bears for Children's Healthcare of Atlanta.

## Helpful Links:

**The Crewe of the Grateful Gluttons:**
http://www.gratefulgluttons.com/traditions.htm

**Centennial Olympic Park Ice Skating:**
http://bit.ly/mxJWAp

**Underground Atlanta St. Patrick's Day Activities:**
http://bit.ly/jKnZ2F

# Activities Index

# Acknowledgements:

**Cover Art:** Ashley Lenz, Lenz Design

**Editing:** Jeff Nystrom and Leigh Ann Livaditis

**Formatting and Web Design:** Ben Hanna

## About the Author

Sue Rodman is a resident of Atlanta and the mother of three boys, ages 13, 11 and 7. She is also the Editor and Publisher of Field Trips with Sue, an award winning blog about things to do with kids in Atlanta and the Southeast. The blog is a Nickelodeon Parent's Pick winner and a featured blog on Raveable.com, (named by Travel + Leisure magazine as a top travel site). The blog is also featured on ATL Insider (the website of the Atlanta Convention and Visitor's Bureau) and has featured posts on national travel sites, Travel Savvy Mom and Best Family Travel Advice. Bi-monthly, see Field Trips with Sue segments on CBS Better Mornings Atlanta. Sue has also appeared on the local Atlanta NBC affiliate, 11 Alive.

When not scouting new adventures, Sue is an award winning marketing and public relations professional. She is an experienced agency executive with international, as well as boutique firms. She has managed successful campaigns for national brands, mid-sized companies, small start-ups, and trade associations including: Feld Entertainment(creators of Disney on Ice, Ringling Bros. & Barnum and Bailey Circus, Monster Jam and Nuclear Cowboyz), Allconnect, Atlantic Station LLC, and the Georgia Press Association. In her spare time, she serves on the marketing committee at Imagine It! The Children's Museum of Atlanta and volunteers at her sons' elementary school, as well as serving as vice president communications for the Sutton Middle School PTA.

# Contact Field Trips with Sue

**email:** sue@fieldtripswithsue.com

**Twitter:** @suerodman

**Facebook:** www.facebook.com/fieldtripswithsue

**Youtube:** www.youtube.com/suerodman

**Linkedin:** www.linkedin/in/suerodman

Made in the USA
Lexington, KY
28 August 2013